Grades 3-5

MW01182116

THE
SUBMARINE BIRD

THE
SUBMARINE BIRD

words by JACK DENTON SCOTT

photographs by OZZIE SWEET

G. P. PUTNAM'S SONS / NEW YORK

Our appreciation to John Hamlet, without whose interest
and help the underwater photography in this book would
not have been possible.

Published simultaneously in Canada
by Academic Press Canada Limited, Toronto.
(formerly Longman Canada Limited)
Printed in the United States of America.
Book design by Bobye List.
Library of Congress Cataloging in Publication Data
Scott, Jack Denton
The submarine bird.
Summary: Discusses the life cycle and habits of cormorants,
web-footed birds that catch fish by diving underwater.
1. Cormorants—Juvenile literature.
|1. Cormorants| I. Sweet, Ozzie. II. Title.
QL696.P4745.S36 1980 598.4'3 79-18297
ISBN 0-399-20701-5

. . . such is the astonishing diving and submerging power of
the cormorant, that this unique bird has been caught in fishing nets
over 200 feet beneath the surface of the sea . . .

NEWLY HATCHED, SCALY-NECKED, BEADY-EYED cormorants look strikingly like diamondback rattlesnakes.

Probably more than any other bird, the cormorant, especially when young, offers remarkable physical proof of the accepted theory that birds evolved from reptiles.

Over 150 million years ago in the Jurassic age reptiles dominated life on earth. There were 16 groups, some of them giant-sized, including flying pterodactyls and marine plesiosaurs, the long-necked swamp dwellers. It is believed that these reptiles came from a more ancient and primitive group that existed even before this age of the dinosaurs and their grotesque-looking, flying cousins.

That period, 200 million years ago, was the Triassic, and the only creatures that lived then were lizardlike tree climbers. Gradually they developed long, loose scales, some of which began to fringe their bodies. This gave them an advantage: The longer scales with splitting, fraying edges made it easier to glide from one branch to another. These crawling reptiles, whose scales were slowly making that metamorphosis to feathers, were the forebears of both the dinosaurs and birds that lumbered into life about 50 million years later. The birds continued their astonishing development after the decline of the great reptiles.

Scientists found similarities between bird and dinosaur, and its later relative, the crocodile. Their jaws, necks, legs, and rib structures had some features in common. Their brain cases were similar. They both had scales; they both laid eggs.

But that spectacular leap from land-bound reptile to feathered, free-flying bird had never been completely explained scientifically or proved until about 100 years ago. At that time archaeologists unearthed an amazing discovery: the prototype of the bird.

In a 150-million-year-old bed of limestone in Bavaria, Germany, three birdlike fossilized bodies, about the size of crows, were found. Named *Archaeopteryx* (meaning ancient wing), the fossils bore the imprint of true feathers. From that discovery, scientists traced the beginning of changes in the bodies of these first birds. Spines grew, ribs fused, bones became light and hollow.

Later, an even more conclusive discovery was made. In rocks laid down in the Cretaceous period of 100 million years ago, fossils were found that clearly resembled the cormorant. That makes the cormorant among the most ancient of Aves, the class all birds belong to, which is made up of twenty-seven orders and 9,000 species.

Watching today's cormorant peck its way to life through the tough eggshell with its egg tooth is to take an imaginery trip back in time and envision their evolution. As the baby bird struggles, squirming snakelike from the shell barrier to freedom, it seems to be in that early primitive bird form, with signs of the old reptile ancestors still stamped upon it.

At birth, the cormorant is indeed a throwback to prehistoric times, actually resembling that first bird, the *Archaeopteryx*. The cormorants in this nest are believed to be almost the same as they were 40 million years ago.

But the cormorant is an unusual bird that has adapted to the modern world as well as some of its more sophisticated relatives, and better than many of the species among the 100 billion birds in existence today. A superb swimmer, diver, and fisherman, and a flyer of note, the cormorant has survived through the ages to become one of the hardiest and most unique birds alive. It is one of the few with equal mastery of both air and water.

The shells from which the taut, naked, blue-skinned young were born began with a light bluish or greenish hue. Before the pecking began, they acquired a chalky covering. Numbering from two to four, rarely as many as seven, the fertilized eggs are the result of a three-year-old male anxiously seeking his first mate.

On the ground, out on a limb, or up in the sky, the young male keeps a constant lookout for a female that pleases him. When he finds her, he uses various displays in his attempts to attract her.

He will perform antics in the water, spreading his wings wide and sailboating along, or he will skillfully dive, then pop up like a cork. Often he will make a deep dive to get rockweed, which he tosses into the air, catches, and presents to the female. Or he will soar like an eagle, gain altitude, and dive, wings whistling.

The male always tries to attract the most mature-plumaged female, and she in turn responds to the male that sings the most maturely. Sometimes a group of young males will sit on the same limb of a stunted tree near the sea, and sing to attract females, the song a low, continuous *ok ok ok ok ok ok,* for about an hour at thirty-second intervals, the sounds audible up to 200 yards away. If there are several males singing for one female, one by one they will drop out of the contest, leaving the field to the male that continues his lusty croaking without stopping.

Once the male has captured the attention of a female, he flies to his nest site and entices her to him with more song and fancy wing action.

When she arrives, the song ceases, and the male moves his head in a snakelike movement, mouth open, making clicking sounds with each forward motion of his head. The female responds with the same head motion but utters no sound. Still twisting his neck, the male croaks, and touches her beak. She responds again, then both caress heads, beaks, and necks. The pair-formation bond has been made.

Actual copulation or breeding is usually accomplished in the nest. That nest is not a work of art. Coarsely woven of twigs, sticks, grass, feathers, and seaweed, it takes them about four days to complete.

Because these are submarine birds that explore the world beneath the sea's surface, sometimes the nest contains strange objects.

In "Audubon's Labrador," Dr. Charles Townsend wrote about a trading schooner that was sunk off the Labrador coast. "This summer," he wrote, "when some fishermen visited a cormorant island nearby, they found that the birds had decorated their nests with pocket-knives, pipes, hairpins, and ladies' combs—objects which the cormorants had obtained by diving to the wreck."

If it is an old nest, the pair rebuild it in about two days, laying on a new top and adding lining. A new nest is about two feet in diameter and two or three inches high. Both birds bring the material, dropping it upon the site. When the pile seems large enough they start shaping it, roughly weaving it and building up the sides. The female decides when it is ready by snuggling into it, restlessly moving around, and tucking material around her. The male constantly adds new nesting, which the female incorporates into the nest.

Once they start collecting for the nest the area is never unguarded, for stealing the nesting is common among cormorants, which some ornithologists point out as a mark of intelligence.

The nest site, if well selected, always includes a nearby perch for the bird that is off duty. The pair defend their territory by displays of intimidation, seldom by actual combat. But the displays can be aggressive, with hissing, wing-striking, and dagger thrusts of their beaks.

Dates when eggs are actually laid vary according to the location. In Florida, where there is a permanent colony of cormorants, they are deposited in the nests almost year round—from late December to late October. Off the coast of Maine, cormorants lay their eggs from mid-May to mid-July when the birds migrate there from southern climates.

Both birds incubate the eggs, usually after the third egg is laid, occasionally earlier. For the first few days the female spends more time on the nest. The incubation span is made up of one- to three-hour periods, depending upon the birds. Observers have found that some males are lazy and put the greater work load on the female; others have seen these roles reversed. Whichever bird is on the nest when darkness falls is there for the night, the other standing guard.

The eggs must be kept at a relatively high temperature or the embryos will not develop. Most species of birds have hormones that grow "brood patches" of bare skin which transfer heat to the clutch of eggs. But cormorants use their highly vascular feet to keep the eggs warm. The incubation period is about twenty-five days. Hatching time runs from two to four days.

After her offspring have emerged, the female tosses the shells out of the nest. Both parents feed the newly hatched chicks with semiliquid food from the lower bill, pumping it directly into their mouths. Even though the naked chick's eyes do not open for four days, by the second day they are pushing their beaks into the open mouths of the parents.

The sound now from the nestlings is a constant peeping for food. The sight in the nest is one of gaping mouths. In fact, a chick in its early stages is one big, begging mouth.

They are fed six times a day, with the concentration in the late morning and early afternoon.

The chicks are brooded in shifts by the parents for about two weeks. But even after that time they are sheltered from wind, rain, and too strong sunlight by the adult birds spreading their wings to protect them.

Changing the guard at the nest is a somewhat formal procedure. The bird returning to take over the incubation or brooding chores bows to its mate, circles it, then gently caresses the head of the brooding bird with its beak, often sliding its head under its body. After this ceremony, the bird leaves the nest and walks away without a backward glance as the other climbs in.

The young are brooded constantly until the sixth day when dark brown, cottony down begins to cover their nakedness. It grows fast, first appearing on the wings and sides and behind the legs, then on the back, rump, shanks, and lower belly. The dark down then starts to grow all over the body, but remains sparse under the wings. It grows in tufts, some small, some large. By the end of the second week the nestlings are completely covered with black wool-like down.

On the nineteenth day flight feathers appear, bursting from sheaths. In four more days wing quills break through, and at twenty-eight days, body feathers begin to blossom.

Pampered by their parents, the chicks grow fast. At about nine days they can stand up in the nest and are clamoring for food almost constantly, even though they are fed regularly and diligently.

As the young grow, the early diet is changed gradually to more solid food, until finally they can manage small pieces of fish. The fastest increase in their size comes during the periods from six to nine days and from eleven to fourteen days. At these times, observers say one can almost see them grow, the change is so rapid.

At two weeks of age they stand most of the time and become more independent of their parents, except at feeding times. There is little or no brooding now, but the parents do appear occasionally to protect them from heavy rains and strong sun. The birds are alone in the nest, raucous and wobbly, with some of them falling out.

They remain black nestlings, but the reptile look is fading and is replaced by an almost vulturelike appearance.

By the third week the nest is all activity. The young cormorants trample over one another, exercise their wings, and have a new cry, an appeased call after feeding, *cuk-hor-hor-hor-hor-hor.*

Now they excrete over the side of the nest, play, have mock fights, and sleep after meals. They can use their beaks, which have begun to elongate and hook slightly, to snap at other, slightly older birds that approach their nest.

By the end of three weeks, the young have outgrown the nest. They peer skyward, restless. One by one they start to leave, returning only at feeding time.

Not yet flying, at first they wander only short distances, but before they are a month old they join other fledglings and wander in small bands around the cormorant community. At five weeks they may have joined a band of as many as forty juvenile birds. They begin to act independently, forsaking their parents and their nest area except at feeding time, when they rush back and beg food.

They can dive well at one month and fly at about five and a half or six weeks. As soon as they take to the air successfully and fly to water, the nest site is abandoned completely as a feeding station.

At seven weeks they take clumsy flights from water and go with the adults, watching and learning the techniques of diving and fishing. At seven and a half weeks they have become expert swimmers and spend much time in the water, cavorting and diving. They will boldly beg food from their parents anywhere in the community and at night roost anyplace other adults will permit.

In another week they fly strongly enough to make long journeys with the flock, but until they are nine weeks old they still haven't broken the old habit of being fed by their parents, and continue to beg food from them at every opportunity.

Fully independent at ten weeks, they finally feed themselves, roost where they please, and associate almost exclusively with other cormorants their own age. All of the fuzzy black down has disappeared.

It will take two years, however, for the dusky-brown, undistinguished juvenile birds to acquire complete adult plumage, transforming them into handsome, sleek representatives of a most unusual seabird clan, the suborder Pelecani, to which another ancient bird, the pelican, also belongs.

At that time they will become full-fledged members of a great waterbird family, the Phalacrocoracidae, of the Pelecaniformes order. In simpler language, at two years of age the birds will be readily identified as double-crested cormorants, the most popular species. Their name comes from the double crest of long, uncurled, black and white crown feathers at each side of the head, grown for a brief period during the mating season. However, some of the mating birds do not carry the crest at all.

One of thirty cormorant species, the birds here are all double-crested (with three subspecies). They are often seen off the New England coast, in Florida, and on many lakes and large rivers. The three subspecies are the Florida cormorant (actually a double-crested that is a permanent resident of Florida), the white-crested, and the Farallan.

The double-crested cormorant ranges widely along the coasts, from Alaska and the Aleutians to southern California, and from Newfoundland to Florida, the Bahamas, and Cuba. Inland, it is seen from southern Washington to southern California, and from the Prairie Provinces of Canada to Utah, Nebraska, and the region of the Great Lakes. In winter, these inland birds move to rocky islands off the seacoasts and finally migrate south. The cormorant in all species is so adaptable that it has spread to most parts of the world. But our bird, the double-crested, is resident only in North America.

Its adult plumage is distinctive, with its head, neck, and underparts shiny black with a slight greenish gloss, and its upperparts and mantle black with a bronze cast. Its feathers have wide, shiny black margins and black shafts, giving it a scaled look. A narrow line around the eyes is dotted a bright blue. A dull to bright orange skin pouch hangs below the bill.

From a distance cormorants resemble small geese or large, long-necked ducks, but their heads are smaller, their bills hooked, slender, and compressed, and their necks long and snaky. Ranging in length from twenty-nine to thirty-six inches, males and females look exactly alike, with the female somewhat smaller.

These are among the most social of all birds, breeding and living in colonies, mainly on small, rocky, isolated islands. The cormorants here were in residence in an island cluster called the Isle of Shoals, ten miles off the coast of Maine.

Typical cormorant country, it is a place of ocean, sky, and rock. Hundreds of birds gather here to mate, breed, and raise their young, often staying until late October when the entire congregation is ready to fly south. They often return to the breeding islands as early as April.

Cormorants are so well adjusted socially that 10,000 birds gathered in one community is not unusual and three times that many is not rare. Nests are built so closely together that the island looks like one gigantic nest. The only conflict that sometimes occurs is when a mate is lured away by another cormorant.

These islands are ideally located, for they offer an undisturbed site and a convenient food supply. Cormorants are particular about such locations, limiting food foraging to under ten miles from the colony.

Rookeries come alive at dawn. The rustling of feathers, hoarse gruntings, and some sounds resembling coughing signal that the colony is about to begin its day. Time is spent foraging for fish, feeding the young, perching on rocks, drowsing, often sitting with wings outstretched. On the water beneath the rocky outcropping, the young frolic in swimming and diving practice sessions.

It appears a peaceful scene, for cormorants have few enemies, especially in these isolated islands.

But the one enemy they do have is always near.

Great black-backed and herring gulls periodically swoop over the island looking for unattended young and eggs in nests. It is rare that they find any, for cormorants are attentive parents, and usually one is on guard. Cormorants give bullfroglike alarm calls when gulls appear. Gulls, large as they are, usually permit the much smaller cormorants to drive them away from nests.

But the gulls are resourceful. Often they nest right in the cormorant rookery, raising their chicks, stealing food from the cormorants, and gobbling their young and eggs whenever they can. Alert, fast, and bold, the great black-backed gulls sometimes even take food intended for their young from adult cormorants.

Largely, though, it is a live-and-let-live society, with cormorants and gulls coexisting. But it is a forced coexistence and there isn't much the cormorants can do about it. Their armor is vigilance, and mainly it seems effective. And gulls do improve cormorant breeding by eliminating the weak and ill.

In Florida, cormorants live in complete harmony with the wading birds, even fishing in the shallows with pelicans, and peacefully sharing fishing and roosting places with egrets, herons, storks, and pelicans.

In the South, they also fly in mixed groups with other water birds, sometimes on the way to fishing grounds, often just exercising. However, the flight of the cormorant is unmistakable. The neck is stretched, the head slightly raised, the feet pointed straight behind and under the flat wedge-shaped tail. The wing beats are steady, with only occasional short glides. Unless on migration, when the flight is V-shaped and high, as it is with geese, they fly close to the surface of the water. They do not seem to be moving fast, but their flight is powerful and has been clocked at forty-eight miles an hour with no wind. But their speed is usually about one half of that.

That flight of cormorants close to the surface of the water has convinced some observers, especially along the North Atlantic shore, that they have seen a mythical creature. For when these dark birds pass diagonally at a distance close to the waves, their long wings appear to overlap, all rising and falling very nearly together in a long line. In the shimmering haze, which weaves a deceptive veil, this can make even the most skeptical persons believe that they are seeing the long folds of a sea serpent slithering through the waves. At least this is how some marine scientists have explained the numerous sightings of sea serpents reported through the years.

It isn't easy for a cormorant to get aloft, nor is it graceful while taking to the air. Taking off from water, it makes a long, upwind run, flapping furiously and vigorously splashing the water, both feet simultaneously striking the water in push-off motion.

Always facing into the wind to get additional lift off the water, it appears to be actually running across the surface before laboriously becoming airborne, not unlike an overloaded amphibious aircraft.

Even after takeoff it gains altitude slowly, with the barely air-borne bird skimming the water, wings flapping steadily in heavy, machinelike motion. Once lift is attained by this hard flying, the cormorant catches the thermals, which are rising bodies of warm air. Then the flight accelerates, the wings appearing to reach out and control the air. Now the flying is graceful and the bird seems a natural part of the upper element. All of the clumsy preflight efforts are replaced with proficient aerial maneuvering.

Cormorants like to take to the air from high vantage positions, such as perches, pilings, limbs of trees, and cliffsides. They actually dive into flight from these heights, falling down until the strong wing motion churns them upward. Because they are heavy birds, with some males weighing just under five pounds, there is not much soaring or gliding even with a wingspan that can reach fifty-two inches. Almost constant flapping is necessary to produce the thrust to keep them airborne. Cormorants are serious, no-nonsense flyers, never exhibiting the aerial acrobatics of some other seabirds, such as gulls. When aloft, they usually are foraging for food or traveling to a destination.

When cormorants are not traveling or foraging or feeding their young, they often spend time roosting in high places, getting the sun, drying their feathers after swimming or fishing.

Unlike most seabirds, cormorants have flight feathers that are permeable, permitting water to pass through and wet them right to the skin. They are not as well waterproofed with natural oils and tight overlapping feathers as ducks. Thus, cormorants are often seen on trees, high rock croppings, or pilings, with their wings extended, looking like vampires with spreading black cloaks.

Some observers, however, have seen cormorants in the wing-drying position during a rainstorm, so they obviously were not spreading their wings to dry them. A few ornithologists attribute this to balance. The cormorant is an accomplished flyer and swimmer, but with the short legs located at the back of their bodies making them unsteady and clumsy when walking, they are far from being perching birds. One expert, after examining a cormorant's skeleton and center of gravity, concluded that it is not well balanced in a perching position with wings folded. He believed that spreading the wings distributed the weight more evenly and aided the cormorant in keeping its balance.

So there are two schools of thought on the dramatic spreading of the cormorant's wings. They do need to dry their feathers, and they may need help in balancing when not in the water or flying. Whatever the correct conclusion, the cormorant, as the watermen say, seems to be "drying his sails."

Another bird, the anhinga, has the same wing-spreading habit and is often confused with the cormorant. They are closely related, but physically quite different. The cormorant has a shorter, hooked bill, the anhinga's is longer, stilettolike. The anhinga's head is slimmer, the neck and tail much longer. The anhinga also has coin-silver spots on its head, neck, back, and wings, and a distinct white band on its wings and the tip of its tail. The anhinga female is easily identified by a buff-colored head, neck, and breast. Also, anhingas inhabit only fresh water. They are never seen around the sea.

For its main role in life, our submarine bird is sheer physical perfection from bill to tail. As a diver and fisherman, it is peerless. Its eyesight is not only superb, but the eyes are positioned in such a manner that the cormorant can look straight down into fishing waters without changing the direction or position of its head.

Although it may locate fish while flying, the cormorant, unlike pelicans and some other diving birds, does not dive after its prey from the air. It always lands on the water, swimming and maneuvering, locating fish with its keen eyesight before bringing its marvelous skills into play.

The bill, sharply hooked at the end, helps in the capture of prey; the serrated edges aid the cormorant in firmly grasping the slippery fish.

Like a submarine, the cormorant can alter its specific gravity, shift and expel internally stored air to change buoyancy. Thus, at one moment it may be floating high on the water, and the next rapidly sink with scarcely a ripple. This remarkable ability has two assets: It enables the bird to stalk prey effectively underwater, and helps it to disappear quickly and to escape from danger.

The cormorant also lacks the normal water bird's air sacs under the skin, and its bones are much heavier than the other birds that make their living from the water. But these differences are not detrimental. Lacking those air sacs and light bones, which give buoyancy, the cormorant can submerge and dive very fast.

As an additional aid, the submarine bird can also close its hatch and use its periscope: Its nostrils are closed, and its eyes are adapted for underwater vision. Unlike most vertebrates, it can vary the shape of both lens and cornea to compensate for distorting underwater refraction.

The cormorant's twelve tail feathers are stiff, acting as an effective rudder, and for its size it has larger webbed feet than any other bird, the broad web stretching across all four toes.

It is a fact that fish can swim swiftly—but only for a short distance. They tire quickly and the cormorant has learned this.

Spotting a fish from the surface, the cormorant either plunges forward, quickly arrowing underwater, or slowly and stealthily submerges. It swims with neck extended, using only the strong webbed feet—unless it needs an extra burst of speed. Then it actually flaps its wings, propelling itself swiftly through the water. With such speed from webbed feet and "flying" wings, few fish can outdistance it.

With its sharp "fishhook" bill it grabs its prey and surfaces, then carefully positions the fish and gulps it down headfirst so barbs and fins do not impede swallowing.

Other cormorants that haven't been lucky or skillful enough to catch their own fish are usually around and alert for a slip. If the successful bird loses its crippled fish, even for a moment, it may never see it again.

Unless it is feeding young, the cormorant usually is satisfied with about a pound of fish a day and only needs about a half hour of fishing time to obtain it. Its skill is so great, however, that when it runs into a school of small fish it can get carried away. The crop and gullet of one cormorant obtained for research purposes held the remains of seventy-six four-inch-long anchovies.

In the clear water of lakes, observers have seen this remarkable fisherman at work. Birdman Dr. P. L. Hatch, watching the submarine activities of cormorants in Minnesota lakes, remarked, "Being principally fish eaters they spend most of the time in the water where their movements in pursuit of prey are simply marvelous in velocity. With their totipalmated feet folded flatly into mere blades while carried forward, and when struck out backward opening to their utmost, and half-spread wings beating with inconceivable rapidity, they seem to actually fly through the waters at various depths."

It was once believed that cormorants hunted mainly by sight. But some scientists have observed them fishing in rivers so muddy that any vision underwater would appear to be impossible. So they added hearing to the cormorant's fishing skills. This theory was substantiated when one cormorant, caught in a fishing net, in superb physical condition, was found to be totally blind.

This impressive fishing skill was observed, admired, and envied by human fishermen, until, centuries ago, no one is certain when, some ingenious person decided to utilize the cormorant's ability for the benefit of man. Historians trace it back to 1000 B.C., but think that it was probably an ancient sport even then.

Thus, for hundreds of years fishermen in China, India, and Japan used cormorants instead of fishing rods, traps, or even nets.

Japan is most famous for its trained fishing cormorants, but the Chinese were perhaps the most skillful and patient in the training process. They not only raised their cormorants in captivity, beginning with the eggs, but even developed their own strains of birds, selecting and pairing the most skillful and enthusiastic. The Chinese placed the eggs from these special breedings under broody hens and fed the fledglings eels' blood, according to Friar Odoric, a missionary to China, who observed and wrote about the cormorant fisheries in the fourteenth century. He also may have given the birds their name, calling them *corbeaus marins,* or "water crows," from which evolved the word "cormorant."

When the young, tame birds (that had not been taught by parent birds as they would have been in the wild) began to take an interest in swimming, the Chinese would tie long cords on them near a pond or lake. Their trainer would then toss small dead fish near them into shallow water. When he threw the fish, the trainer whistled shrilly, a "fetch" signal. As the bird caught the fish, the whistle-signal changed in tone and meaning to bring back, or retrieve. If the bird cooperated it was quickly fed good fresh "reward" fish.

According to American writer Dan Mannix, who himself has trained and fished with cormorants, a flock of Chinese cormorants thus trained would "have put a well-trained pack of foxhounds to shame." He recorded that upon finding a school of fish, the Chinese cormorants would surround it. Then, without breaking that ring, they would dart in, catching fish as they moved forward, narrowing the circle. As a bird returned to its boat to deposit a captured fish, his place was filled by another waiting bird. So well trained were these birds that, if one was inattentive and got out of the line surrounding the fish, the rest of the cormorants would make loud guttural sounds and beat the water with their wings until that bird got back into its proper position.

Early accounts assert that these Oriental cormorants were so obedient that they would swim back to their boat and disgorge the fish without assistance from their trainer, depositing them in their own baskets. One large cormorant was always the leader on each boat, or fishing flock, and would attack lazy or inept birds, keeping them at work. Mannix claims that the Japanese called this bird *Ichi,* or "the boss."

Other accounts, later than Friar Odoric's, describe the Chinese birds less dramatically. Working with several boats, deployed in an advancing crescent formation, the fishermen drove their flocks before them upon a school of fish. It appears that the fishermen planned the strategy, not the birds.

Each fisherman recognized his own birds, even though to the unpracticed eye they all looked exactly alike. In turn, each cormorant knew its own boat, and even its own perching station on the boat. There was remarkable teamwork among the trained birds. If one cormorant caught a fish too large to handle, the other birds from that boat rushed to help. They subdued, sometimes killed the fish, but the bird that originally caught the fish was always the one that returned it to the boat.

The birds wore hemp collars at the base of the neck that prevented them from swallowing the fish that they so expertly caught. Trained to return captured fish to the boat, they were given reward food, a gullet full of fresh fish after their workday was finished.

So respected were the fishing cormorants in China that special firms bred and trained them commercially, selling them to the highest bidders, after the birds' abilities were demonstrated. It was a sound investment. The trained birds averaged an eighteen-year life span, some living even longer.

The Japanese worked somewhat differently. Each fisherman had a dozen cormorants, each bird on a long leather leash. The birds perched on the bow of the boat, which had hanging from it an open metal basket in which faggots were burned for light, and also to attract fish. The Japanese fished at dusk, floating downstream, working the birds on their long leather tethers, their necks encircled by a tight leather thong. As each bird filled its throat with small fish, or caught a large one, it was pulled aboard the boat, the fish taken from it, and the bird again placed in the water. As with the Chinese method, at the end of each fishing day each bird was fed a throatful of fish, the constricting thong removed so the reward fish could be swallowed.

However, after packing the birds' throats with fish, the Japanese retied the leather thong above the fish, otherwise the birds would disgorge them, so conditioned were they to giving up their catches when they were hauled back to the boat.

Modern fishing methods make cormorant fishing uneconomical, although, like falconry, it is still practiced by some, mainly for sport, in China, Japan, India, Europe, and the United States.

In Japan it is presently kept alive by the Imperial Household, both for its cultural interest and as a dramatic tourist attraction. The Imperial Household subsidizes an ancient guild of cormorant fishermen on the Nagara River at Gifu that still carries on the ancient art in all of its medieval trappings. Gifu fishermen do not train the so-called Common Cormorant that nests throughout Honshu, which rival fishermen on the Tamagawa River use. They work exclusively with the larger Sea Cormorant of Japan, which a special guild of birdlimers catches for them on the sea cliffs of northeastern Honshu. Some believe that this big bird is more difficult to train, but the men from Gifu claim that it is worth the extra effort, for the Sea Cormorant's throat holds larger fish, thus offering a more dramatic sight to the observers who flock to watch these fascinating birds at work.

Modern fishermen have also envied the cormorant's abilities, and accused the unique bird of catching fish valuable to man.

Thus, at one period, the double-crested cormorant was seriously endangered, with fishermen and hunters shooting them at every opportunity. But the so-called ''fish-stealers'' actually took only a small amount of our food fish.

Biologists examined hundreds of cormorant catches and discovered that mainly the "master fishermen" preyed upon "trash" fish—stickleback, silverside, gunnel, rosefish, blenny, sculpin, sand launce, butterfish, wrasse, sea catfish, dace, and carp. None was fish valued by man.

During his research one biologist observed a flock of cormorants fishing in concert in San Francisco Bay, using a technique similar to the old Chinese method.

Several flying flocks, attracted by a number of cormorants diving and fishing, landed immediately without circling, and formed a long, narrow, closely packed line. Fifty birds swam in a single line; the entire fishing fleet consisted of about 500, three or four birds deep. The fishing was done by the front rank, with the birds diving, swimming forward, then resurfacing, usually in the same position as the line continued to move forward.

If a fishing cormorant surfaced behind the line, it flew ahead, landed on the water, and waited for the line of working birds to catch up. About thirty percent were underwater at one time. It was all very efficient; at least 100 of the surfacing birds had fish. When appetites were satisfied, the impressive teamwork ceased and the large flock broke up, birds scattering on the water, eventually all taking to the air and returning to their own colonies.

That biologist used one word to sum up America's sleek, smart submarine bird. *Spectacular!*

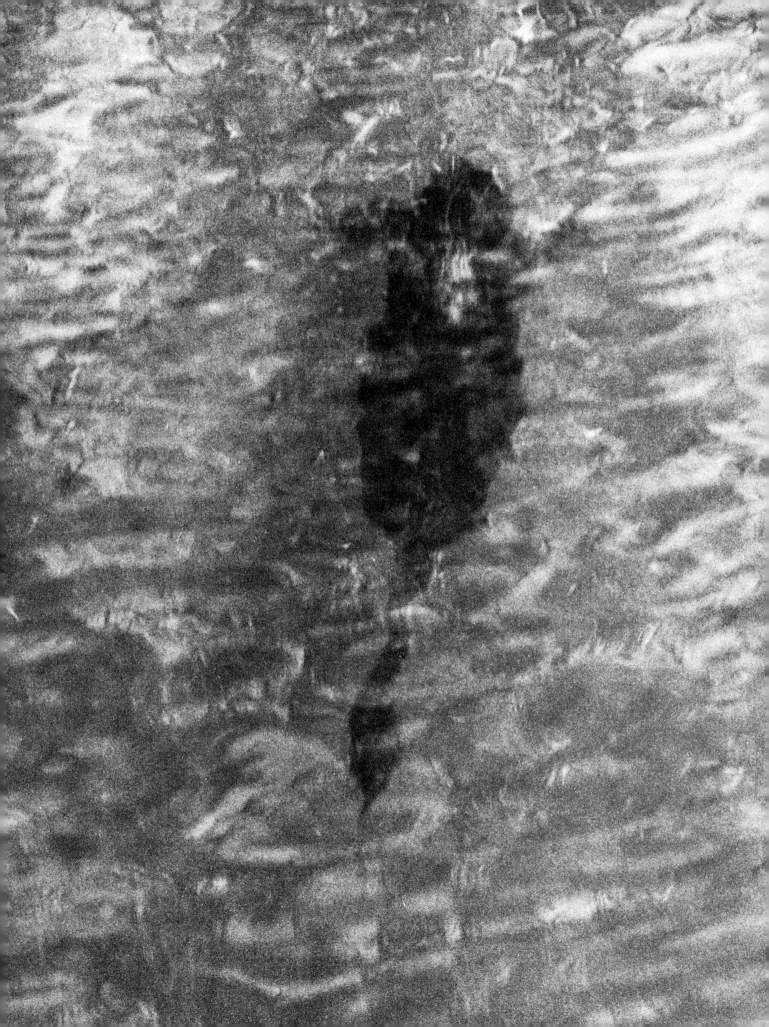

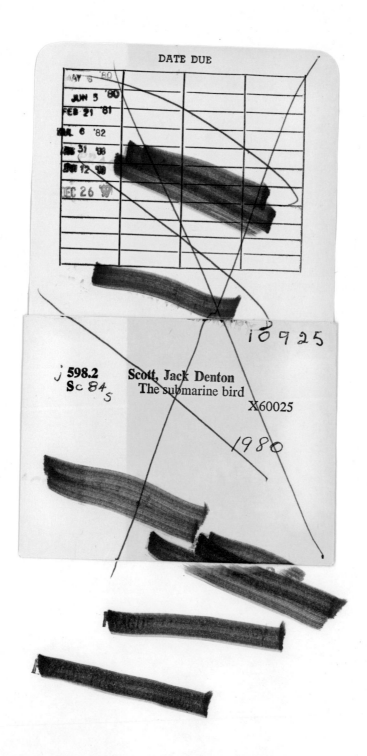